Copyright ©
Donald PH.D

All rights reserved. No part of this publication may be reproduced, distributed, or transmitted in any form or by any means, including photocopying, recording, or other electronic or mechanical methods, without the prior written permission of the publisher, except in the case of brief quotation embodied in critical reviews and certain other non-commercial uses permitted by copyright law.

Contents

Presentation 4
Understanding "Fungibility" 10
What Is an NFT? 11
Pros and Cons of Non-Fungible Tokens 17
Uses of Non-Fungible Tokens 18
Why do they have value? 24
What makes NFTs so exciting? 25
What makes NFTs so popular? 27
Trends in the NFT industry 28
Best NFT projects: 10 projects to keep on your radar ... 29
What are some of the upcoming NFTs that could become the next hit? 38
Tips for Investing 39
Is Investing in NFTs Worth It? 41
How to Invest in NFTs 50
How Is an NFT Different from Cryptocurrency? 53
How Does an NFT Work? 54
How to make money with non-fungible tokens (NFTs) ... 56
How to Buy NFTs 58
Popular NFT Marketplaces 60
Should You Buy NFTs? 63
The Opportunities With NFTs 66

Are NFT Stocks The Right Investment For You? 67
Advantage of Non-Fungible Tokens 69
Disadvantages 71
End 73

Presentation

Non-fungible tokens (NFTs) seem to have burst out of the ether this year. From workmanship and music to tacos and tissue, these advanced assets are selling like seventeenth century extraordinary Dutch tulips some for millions of dollars. In any case, are NFTs worth the money or the hype? Some experts say they're a bubble ready to pop, like the dotcom frenzy or Beanie Babies. Others trust NFTs are here to stay, and that they will change investing forever.

The latest theoretical air pocket brought to you by Bitcoin and its underlying blockchain innovation is NFT workmanship non-fungible tokens that are applied towards art and collectables. Non-fungible products are remarkable and authentic registers of a limited-edition collectable item, such as an uncommon baseball card or a numbered craftsmanship print. They supposedly cannot be counterfeited, making them a structure of currency appended to the value of the item.

When you purchase or sell NFT art, you don't own content or a work of workmanship; rather you own the rights to the remarkable token on the blockchain. You don't control the rights to its replication or distribution. Although people have since quite a while ago utilized art to store value, crypto easily extends the concept into digitized and tokenised craftsmanship, making it proficient to also move value. It addresses an advanced and present day platform for putting in workmanship and using it in the same way that someone may trade gold, stocks or bitcoin. To date, NFTs have produced billions of dollars of turnover: One NFT Everydays: The First 5,000 Days, by the American advanced artist known as Beeple as of late sold at Christie's for nearly US$70 million. Indeed, agreeing to information from the NFT stage CryptoSlam, people spent more than $1 billion on digital assets in April alone.

Crypto art has been around for about five years, yet for some examiners outside of the crypto world, NFTs detonated out of nowhere. The bubble is being expanded by a number of theoretical factors that include the pandemic, the wild development in bitcoin prices and institutional acknowledgment (as organizations such as Tesla purchase and validate bitcoin). Homebound financial backers furnished with the latest trading platforms have nothing better to do in a pandemic than chase new trends in chatrooms: The next bitcoin; decimating hedge-store short sellers, or foraging for the next bubble.

and excludes more established generations who dread new frontiers that will either change everything. Or on the other hand nothing.

Hypotheses or "madnesses of swarms" take hold when a bubble that appears can bridge the unpretentious nuance between what individuals need and what they truly need. Investors can easily convince themselves about inherent value after buying a phony canvas. Urgency implies that the more you pay for it, the less inclined youare to doubt its validity. Furthermore, you'll wear urgency like cheap cologne.

NFTs are likely to be overinflated at some point, because of so much money, speculators and producers of NFTs are supplying and rushing into this space. Digital tokens work on the same principles as their crypto-currency relatives. They can't be duplicated, they can be easily verified and confirmed on the blockchain, and they are immutable. Yet this is no chance to be sure they'll maintain their intrinsic value over time. Value is currently only driven by shortage. As with any speculative frenzy, the key to success and not being consumed by a chaotic collapse is to buy and sell early. Air pockets will fundamentally shame investors because they'll either endure the lament of purchasing too late or selling too early. The main weakness of bitcoin and NFT is that purchasers and sellers still reference them to fiat currency like US dollars, rather than holding them as a separate, reliable store of value and strategy of move.

Understanding "Fungibility"

"Fungibility" is a concept that applies to both real-world and digital assets. It defines something that is replaceable with an identical item. Money is an excellent example. A dollar is always equivalent to a dollar regardless of its serial number and its location (e.g., your wallet, bank account, etc.). Most cryptocurrencies are fungible. They are designed in a way that each individual token is identical to the next one. For instance, one Bitcoin is always equivalent to one Bitcoin. It is equal and interchangeable with all other Bitcoins.

What Is an NFT?

NFT stands for 'non-fungible token'. The name is the most intimidating and confusing thing about NFTs, 'Fungibility' is a simple concept that basically refers to items that you use every day. You can think of these items as being physical money or even bitcoin. For example, since bitcoin is fungible (or identical to) you can trade one for another bitcoin, and you'll have exactly the same thing. 'Non-fungible' (the opposite of fungible) means that it's unique and can't be replaced with something else. A one-of-a-kind trading card is non-fungible, as is the Mona Lisa painting. If you traded either the card or the painting you'd receive something completely different in return.

An NFT is a digital asset that represents real-world objects like art, music, in-game items and videos. They are bought and sold online, frequently with cryptocurrency, and they are generally encoded with the same underlying software as many cryptos. Although they've been around since 2014, NFTs are gaining notoriety now because they are becoming an increasingly popular way to buy and sell digital artwork. A staggering $174 million has been spent on NFTs since November 2017.

NFTs are also generally one of a kind, or at least one of a very limited run, and have unique identifying codes. "Essentially, NFTs create digital scarcity," says Arry Yu, chair of the Washington Technology Industry Association Cascadia Blockchain Council and managing director of Yellow Umbrella Ventures. This stands in stark contrast to most digital creations, which are almost always infinite in supply. Hypothetically, cutting off the supply should raise the value of a given asset, assuming it's in demand. But many NFTs, at least in these early days, have been digital creations that already exist in some form elsewhere, like iconic video clips from NBA games or securitized versions of digital art that's already floating around on Instagram.

For instance, famous digital artist Mike Winklemann, better known as "Beeple" crafted a composite of 5,000 daily drawings to create perhaps the most famous NFT of the moment, "EVERYDAYS: The First 5000 Days," which sold at Christie's for a record-breaking $69.3 million. Anyone can view the individual images—or even the entire collage of images online for free. So why are people willing to spend millions on something they could easily screenshot or download? Because an NFT allows the buyer to own the original item. Not only that, it contains built-in authentication, which serves as proof of ownership. Collectors value those "digital bragging rights" almost more than the item itself.

While NFTs are digital assets such as bitcoin and other cryptocurrencies, they are fundamentally different. Cryptocurrencies are fungible tokens, which means they can be interchanged. Non-fungible tokens are unique assets that only exist for one owner at a given time. Like bitcoin and other cryptocurrencies, NTFs are bought, sold, and held using blockchain technology. If you buy an NFT, you typically hold it in an online account or cryptocurrency wallet. Because it's a digital-only asset, you can't carry it around in your pocket–unless you have a hardware wallet.

NFTs are one of a kind, which make them attractive to investors, blockchain technology providers, and other crypto players. They can represent various assets, such as:

- Crypto collectibles
- Event tickets
- In-game purchases
- Properties
- Real-word investments

NFTs are sold, bought, and traded whole. They cannot be divided into smaller denominations, just as people cannot purchase only a portion of a limited-edition collectible or plane ticket. Their metadata is also unalterable, which means they come with an unquestionable record of what they represent.

Pros and Cons of Non-Fungible Tokens

An NFT allows users to include as many details as they want regarding what it represents. The additional, authenticated information can ultimately elevate the asset's value, as it gives buyers and investors greater confidence over their potential venture. NFTs are also ERC-720 compliant, which means that they meet the technical standard set for smart contracts on the Ethereum blockchain regarding token implementation.

Like any other cryptocurrency, however, NFTs have downsides. According to recent blockchain news, they are not yet as widely used as their fungible counterparts. Users who are not well-versed in developing decentralised applications may have a hard time utilising NFTs.

Uses of Non-Fungible Tokens

With the right customisation and integration, non-fungible tokens can transform various industries by:

Ensuring copyright protection

NFTs allow digital content creators to exhibit their work in virtual spaces without worries of copyright infringement or art theft. They can help artists retain ownership of their creations, earn more, and even set up a recurring profit stream from future sales.

Facilitating secure and efficient in-platform purchases

According to many blockchain technology companies, NFTs are poised to revolutionise the gaming industry. They can enable players to trade in-game items easily, which is prohibited by most popular titles due to the dangers of online transactions.

Simplifying collectible trade

NFTs have the potential to take collectors' items into the 21st century. They can make it possible to purchase tokenised versions of collectibles, such as rare currency, limited edition action figures, and exclusive fan merchandise.

Collectables

NFT tokens fittingly bring the idea of collectables to the digital world and embrace the concept of digital scarcity, which Bitcoin pioneered. Influencers, cryptocurrency exchanges, and related businesses can issue unique tokens to commemorate special events. Recipients can then hold these tokens are memories or possibly resell them on marketplaces. An excellent example of such collectible tokens are the CryptoPunks NFTs issued by Larvos Labs in 2017 for free to users. Many tokens are now being resold for millions of dollars and remain one of the most valuable crypto collectibles to date.

Gaming Economies

Game developers often build exclusive assets into their applications and bar users from transferring them to other players. For such an economy, bringing these assets to a blockchain is an advancement, allowing both players and game developers to manage them transparently.

Digital Identity

Reducing identity theft cases has always been heralded as one of the most prominent use cases for blockchain technology. NFTs bring that use case to life since it allows users to link real-life information such as educational and health credentials to a token. Such a peg would increase uniqueness, privacy, and transparency for others who may need to use such information later.

Asset Tokenization

Distribution of real-world assets such as real estate or building structures could be done with NFTs representing each individual's ownership of the property. These tokens are almost eternally verifiable evidence of the transaction and can be transferred upon repurchase of the property.

Blockchain technology and NFTs afford artists and content creators a unique opportunity to monetize their wares. For example, artists no longer have to rely on galleries or auction houses to sell their art. Instead, the artist can sell it directly to the consumer as an NFT, which also lets them keep more of the profits. In addition, artists can program in royalties so they'll receive a percentage of sales whenever their art is sold to a new owner. This is an attractive feature as artists generally do not receive future proceeds after their art is first sold.

Art isn't the only way to make money with NFTs. Brands like Charmin and Taco Bell have auctioned off themed NFT art to raise funds for charity. Charmin dubbed its offering "NFTP" (non-fungible toilet paper), and Taco

Bell's NFT art sold out in minutes, with the highest bids coming in at 1.5 wrapped ether (WETH) equal to $3,723.83 at time of writing. Nyan Cat, a 2011-era GIF of a cat with a pop-tart body, sold for nearly $600,000 in February. And NBA Top Shot generated more than $500 million in sales as of late March. A single LeBron James highlight NFT fetched more than $200,000. Even celebrities like Snoop Dogg and Lindsay Lohan are jumping on the NFT bandwagon, releasing unique memories, artwork and moments as securitized NFTs.

Why do they have value?

As noted earlier, people used to buy and store collectables such as art, rare stones, comic books, trading cards, and historical value items before the advent of NFTs. The market for art collectable items alone is worth roughly $37 billion. Although these assets may not seem valuable to others, the collector often has a form of attachment to the item that they're willing to put down money on the table for it. Additionally, some NFTs can be resold for a higher price later if someone desires to have the same item because of its uniqueness.

What makes NFTs so exciting?

NFTs have the potential to provide ownership for users that will authenticate their ownership rights. This would allow digital assets to be transferred globally far more easily than any set of collectibles that have come before. Another point is that NFTs provide authenticity, giving buyers confidence when they buy their assets. The use cases for NFTs are only just beginning to be explored. For example, someone may choose to purchase online news articles as NFTs, and while this may seem like a gross indulgence of the super-rich, there are more practical uses that are on their way. Until now, the crypto market has been laser focused on fungible digital assets like bitcoin and Ethereum. NFTs have changed that by providing a marketplace for assets such as digital art, game items, concert tickets, real estate, and more.

What makes NFTs so popular?

NFTs are unique, or non-fungible, digital tokens that run on smart contracts on Ethereum and other blockchains. They can be used to distribute assets and verify their authenticity via the blockchain. The concept of NFTs originated in 2015 and the first projects were launched in 2017. NFTs are being used to sell exclusive items, such as collectibles, online. As each token is unique and cannot be replicated, using NFTs creates scarcity that makes them valuable to collectors as well as artists and other sellers. They are bought and sold in auctions, with payment made in cryptocurrencies such as Ether (ETH) and Bitcoin (BTC). The future of NFTs includes applications in the growing area of decentralised finance

(DeFi), where they can be used to put up valuable assets such as fine art, rare collectibles or even real estate as collateral for loans or as financial contracts for insurance, stock options or bonds.

Trends in the NFT industry

The cryptocurrency boom has created new millionaires looking for other digital assets that hold value to invest their gains. The total traded volume for NFTs in December 2020 was around $12m. The figure soared to well over $500m in March 2021, according to data from NFT blockchain developer Enjin. The best NFT projects in 2021 are involved in selling exclusive and limited-edition items, including digital art, music, trading cards and other collectibles, and attracting eye-watering prices. A series of NFT auctions of digital artworks and music from high-profile artists such as Grimes culminated in a work by the artist Beeple being sold for $69m at Christie's on March 11. New NFT projects are being touted not only as the future of merchandise sales but also a way for musicians to regain ownership of their work in the era of streaming and file sharing, and for game developers to profit from creating in-game economies.

Best NFT projects: 10 projects to keep on your radar

Worldwide Asset eXchange (WAX)

WAX is a decentralised peer-to-peer marketplace for trading NFTs. WAX uses the Delegated Proof of Stake (DPoS) consensus algorithm to maintain security. Developers can build decentralised apps, games and marketplaces on the platform. The WAX token is based on Ethereum and users can earn rewards for staking their tokens to provide liquidity. The WAX token can also be traded on several exchanges, including Huobi, Bittrex and Bancor Network. The token can be stored in any Ethereum-compatible wallet.

CryptoKitties

Launched in 2017 by developer Dapper Labs, it was the CryptoKitties protocol that brought NFTs to the mainstream. It was the first to use the ERC-721 standard, which allows for unique digital assets. In the CryptoKitties game, players raise and resell virtual cats for profit on the Ethereum network. CryptoKitties tokens are non-fungible, each representing a different digital cat. The interest in NFTs has seen a resurgence in interest in the game, which at its height in 2018 saw more than 1 million daily transactions.

Enjin

Enjin was founded in 2009 to develop a gaming network. In 2017, it launched the Enjin Coin (ENJ) and began developing a purpose-build blockchain ecosystem for NFTs. in 2018, Enjin announced one of the world's first gaming multiverses and it now has more than 40 game developers using its platforms to create games. Enjin has grown into an ecosystem of integrated digital products, for trading and monetising games. Developers can use the Enjin Coin to tokenise in-game items on the Ethereum blockchain. In March 2021, Enjin Coin had the highest market cap of all NFTs. More than 1,300 blockchain marketing campaigns have been powered by Enjin's products, gamifying online engagement for companies such as Binance, CoinMarketCap, Kyber Network and CoinGecko. On 31 March, Enjin launched Efinity, its next-generation blockchain for NFTs built on the Polkadot protocol.

Decentraland

Launched in February 2020, Decentraland is a decentralised virtual reality world powered by the Ethereum blockchain that enables users to create and monetise content and applications. Users can purchase plots of virtual land, create customised avatars, participate in governance and trade rare digital collectibles. Users need fungible tokens as well as NFTs to participate in Decentraland. They connect with their crypto wallet through a web browser to set up their avatar, which receives a virtual passport to represent their virtual identity. The Decentraland uses its MANA token, which can be purchased from cryptocurrency exchanges to buy land and in-game assets. Users can also purchase items that are supported on NFT marketplaces.

Rarible

Rarible is an NFT marketplace for creating and trading rare collectibles that was founded in January 2020. The platform supports a wide variety of digital assets, including art, memes, music, domain names and DeFi insurance policies. The creation of NFTs, called minting, is straightforward with an Ethereum wallet and allows artists to release teasers for their content. Rarible gained attention for launching its own governance token, RARI, which is more commonly used in the DeFi space, with a goal of becoming a decentralised autonomous organisation. Rarible is demonstrating ways to integrate NFTs with DeFi, teaming up in September 2020 with Yearn Finance and Nexus Mutual, a blockchain-based insurance platform to provide insurance coverage for NFTs.

NBA Top Shot

Bringing NFTs into the mainstream, the National Basketball Association (NBA) has launched an officially licensed blockchain application for trading collectibles with Dapper Labs. The application is built on the Flow blockchain rather than Ethereum. The Top Shot NFTs contain video clips of memorable game moments and include player statistics as well as information about the NFTs trading history. Limited packs of NFTs are issued weekly, with prices depending on their rarity.

Codex Protocol

Codex is a decentralised title registry secured by blockchain for the verification of authentic NFTs. NFT creators can create a digital record for a collectible that then travels with it, so that prospective buyers can verify its authenticity by checking its identity and ownership history on the Codex Viewer. That creates confidence that collectors are buying authentic products.

OpenSea

Founded in 2017, OpenSea is the largest decentralised NFT marketplace. It lists more than 50 categories of rare assets for trading, including digital art, CryptoKitties, Decentraland and domain names. The platform enables developers to build marketplaces for their digital assets on Ethereum and interoperable standards such as

ERC721 or ERC1155 and earn commission from secondary items. Game developers can build customisable storefronts to automatically trade collectibles.

Ethereum Name Services

The Ethereum Name Services (ENS) domain naming platform was launched in 2017 on the Ethereum blockchain. The domain names are non-fungible and can be integrated into the NFT marketplaces such as Rarible and OpenSea. Users can receive any cryptocurrency, NFT or token to their domain name and launch secure, private and decentralised websites. There are more than 238,000 domain names registered on the platform with more than 71,000 owners.

0xcert

Concluding our list of the top 10 NFT crypto projects, 0xcert is a blockchain application programming interface (API) gateway that allows developers to build decentralised applications using NFTs as well as fungible tokens. Its framework aims to simplify the process of issuing NFTs on the blockchain to reduce development time.

What are some of the upcoming NFTs that could become the next hit?

The potential for the integration of NFTs with DeFi is driving a number of upcoming NFT projects to look out for in the future. They include Unifty, which is an NFT management hub that will feature copyright management and supports multiple blockchains, including Dai, Binance Smart Chain and Polygon. Upshot is a project that will enable the crowdsourcing of appraisals to establish an NFT's value. NFTX will enable the creation of community-owned index funds so that investors can gain exposure to several NFTs through the ownership of one token.

Tips for Investing

If you're interested in blockchain investments but aren't quite ready to trade NFTs or cryptocurrency directly, there's another option. There are a handful of blockchain exchange-traded funds (ETFs) that offer exposure to this emerging technology. Investing in ETFs allows you to own a basket of investments inside a taxable brokerage account and diversify your portfolio without having to join a blockchain marketplace. If you don't have an online brokerage account yet, consider looking for one that offers commission-free trades for stocks and ETFs.

Consider talking to a financial advisor about whether NFTs are something you should be adding to your portfolio. If you don't have a financial advisor yet, finding one doesn't have to be difficult. SmartAsset's financial advisor matching tool makes it easy to connect with professional advisors in your local area. It takes just a few minutes to get your personalized advisor recommendations online.

Is Investing in NFTs Worth It?

NFTs have exploded in popularity. After some investors made millions from NFTs, you may be wondering if you should get in on the hype. Vignesh Sundaresan, the buyer of the $69 million artwork through auction, believes NFTs are a legitimate store of value and represent a shift in how the world views art and collectible assets. In an interview with CNBC, Sundaresan said that NFTs would become a new commodity class that connects buyers and sellers worldwide. However, the NFT he purchased arguably is just a digital image anyone can copy paired with a unique asset address. This has many people skeptical of the value of NTFs. After all, people once thought Beanie Babies and tulips should fetch astronomical price tags. Those fads fell away. Only time will tell if NFTs will hold the value of a Picasso or a pet rock. Even some in the cryptocurrency industry question the value of NFTs. In a thread on Twitter, litecoin founder Charlie Lee says the ability to duplicate the underlying asset negates the value of owning the NFT. He also questions what will happen to the value of the NBA Top Shot Moments if the website goes down, pointing out that physical baseball cards remain valuable long after the manufacturers or leagues cease to exist.

From a certain point of view, the value of NFTs is in the eye of the collector. After all, owning a totally unique object the ultimate criterion for every true collector may be worth nearly any expense if you want it badly enough. But let's say you're not a collector who absolutely must possess the latest digital art work of Beeple, the artist whose EVERYDAYS NFT fetched $69 million, but rather a humble investor who's curious about the potential return on investment of NFTs and their FAANG-like growth. The byword is caution. Think of NFTs like purchasing a vintage sports car or a historic mansion. Without thorough due diligence, it's very hard to know whether you're buying a rare item of value or a lemon that will make you deeply regret taking the plunge. To put it another way, it's very challenging to differentiate between fool's gold and the real deal, especially when the NFT market is in the throes of a massive bubble. But not all NFTs are over-inflated bubble assets, and not all assets caught up in a market bubble are bound to be a bust. Take the dot-com bubble. Sure, there were world-famous losers like Webvan and Pet.com, but there were also gems that delivered outstanding long-term value to those who managed to hold on through the storm or to buy cheap at the bottom. Shares of Amazon peaked at $113 in 1999—and after the bubble burst, they plummeted to

$5.51 in late 2001. Today, Amazon is trading above $3,000 a share.

Another thing is clear about the NFT market: As the popularity of non-fungible tokens boomed in early 2021, their relative scarcity helped them appear quite valuable. But like the podcast craze before them, just about everyone and their mother is coming out with NFTs now. That's making it much more difficult to separate tokens with Amazon-like potential from the hucksters peddling yet another dot-com-era disaster. Given this high level of uncertainty about NFTs valuations, it might be more prudent to take a venture capitalist approach: Don't buy the flavor of the month; rather hedge your bets and invest in a portfolio of assets just like VCs investing in a broad selection of promising startups. Even if you diversify your NFT portfolio by purchasing a variety of tokens, the relatively underdeveloped market may still make it challenging to identify those with long-term growth potential and those that end up as the next Quibi. Given the undeveloped, highly speculative nature of the market, even if you buy many NFTs, it's best to limit your overall NFT exposure to a relatively small percentage of your total portfolio and to be prepared to lose most, if not all, of the money you put in.

Perhaps the most reasonable approach to investing in NFTs, then, is not to consider them investments at all, but to buy tokens that are related to your personal interests or hobbies. If you're a huge Kings of Leon fan, grab up one of the NFTs the band released, including one that offers a set of front-row seats at each tour for life. If you love street art, go forth and collect the hottest new work on Rarible. Own NFTs purely for your own enjoyment, and consider the money spent as a great way to support the artists, players or other creators you care deeply about.

Of course, eventually, the market will separate the wheat from the chaff. And that means that the long-term potential of NFTs is still worth considering. NFTs today are often no more than a digital analog of a real asset. But they could be so much more. Remember newspaper web pages in the early days of the internet? Back in the 1990s, they were nothing more than a delux screenshot of a physical paper, a digital copy of their real-world counterpart. Fast-forward to today. Technological progress means news websites have far more interactive and programmable features than your regular newspaper. That's a similar level of potential that many believe NFTs may possess that they could offer advanced features that aren't readily apparent to us today.

For instance, we already know the blockchain database technology that powers them creates potential anti-fraud applications. Each NFT has a record of its origin and everyone who's ever owned it, which will likely make it easier to spot forgeries going forward. In addition, many NFTs are already turning the payment model for art on its head by providing royalties to artists on each future purchase, which means for the first time many creators will directly benefit from the appreciation of their work over time. But these aspects are just the tip of the proverbial iceberg. As our lives become even more digital-first, there's truly no telling what functionality might emerge that goes well beyond ownership of digital artwork.

Finally, as long as there are people flush with cryptocurrency that is experiencing soaring valuations, it seems obvious that the demand for NFTs will remain elevated. But just like the stock market, it's not always clear what the correct asset is to buy right now. Retail investors motivated by FOMO fear of missing out are throwing money at every investment they can think of in the hope that it turns out to be the next GameStop, Dogecoin or maybe Rembrandt. This wild market suggests that buying NFTs for short-term gains means leaving yourself vulnerable to strong risks of a market crash.

How to Invest in NFTs

If you want to get started with NFTs, you have a few ways to begin. Various NFT platforms allow you to buy, list, and sell specific assets. Depending on the platform, you may need an account there or another form of accepted cryptocurrency wallet. For those who find this process confusing and convoluted, it may be best to avoid NFTs. However,if you're fairly tech-savvy or already have some experience with blockchain-based assets, you should find the process rather straightforward.

Some popular NFT marketplaces include:

- OpenSea
- Rarible
- NBA Top Shot
- Nifty Gateway

Fortunes have been made in the NFT space. There's no guarantee this trend will continue, but current hype and excitement around digital assets have them reaching sky-high prices. If you are thinking about an NFT purchase, consider your risk appetite and evaluate how much money would you be okay losing.

Non-fungible tokens are digital assets a single owner holds. However, others may be able to view and effectively duplicate the asset.

Similar to bitcoin and other cryptocurrencies, NFTs are bought, sold, and stored using blockchains.

Unlike bitcoin and other cryptocurrencies, NFTs cannot be interchanged.

NFTs may increase in value, but they could become worthless. The future of NFTs is highly speculative.

How Is an NFT Different from Cryptocurrency?

NFT stands for non-fungible token. It's generally built using the same kind of programming as cryptocurrency, like Bitcoin or Ethereum, but that's where the similarity ends.

Physical money and cryptocurrencies are "fungible," meaning they can be traded or exchanged for one another. They're also equal in value one dollar is always worth another dollar; one Bitcoin is always equal to another Bitcoin. Crypto's fungibility makes it a trusted means of conducting transactions on the blockchain. NFTs are different. Each has a digital signature that makes it impossible for NFTs to be exchanged for or equal to one another (hence, non-fungible). One NBA Top Shot clip, for example, is not equal to EVERYDAYS simply because they're both NFTs. (One NBA Top Shot clip isn't even necessarily equal to another NBA Top Shot clip, for that matter.)

How Does an NFT Work?

NFTs exist on a blockchain, which is a distributed public ledger that records transactions. You're probably most familiar with blockchain as the underlying process that makes cryptocurrencies possible.

Specifically, NFTs are typically held on the Ethereum blockchain, although other blockchains support them as well.

An NFT is created, or "minted" from digital objects that represent both tangible and intangible items, including:

- Art
- GIFs
- Videos and sports highlights
- Collectibles
- Virtual avatars and video game skins
- Designer sneakers
- Music

Even tweets count. Twitter co-founder Jack Dorsey sold his first ever tweet as an NFT for more than $2.9 million. Essentially, NFTs are like physical collector's items, only digital. So instead of getting an actual oil painting to hang on the wall, the buyer gets a digital file instead. They also get exclusive ownership rights. That's right: NFTs can have only one owner at a time. NFTs' unique data makes it easy to verify their ownership and transfer tokens between owners. The owner or creator can also store specific information inside them. For instance, artists can sign their artwork by including their signature in an NFT's metadata.

How to make money with non-fungible tokens (NFTs)

There are essentially two ways to make money with NFTs.

Minting and Issuing NFTs: If you're an influencer or artist, minting and issuings NFTs to your followers can be an excellent way to earn more income, especially with the hype around the industry. Sites like Rarible and SuperRare offer tools for anyone to mint and sell NFTs. Crypto influencers reported earning thousands of dollars from selling NFTs inspired by the artwork or photographs.

Trading NFTs: You can also make money from buying and selling NFTs on popular marketplaces like OpenSea and Nifty Gateway. While NFTs are not directly exchangeable, some increase in price, making it a potential asset to hold and flip later for a higher price. Additionally, you can follow crypto projects that issue NFTs that are redeemable for crypto or able to sell on a marketplace.

How to Buy NFTs

If you're interested in buying NFTs, you'll first need to locate a blockchain marketplace that sells them. Again, you'll need to have the appropriate cryptocurrency for that marketplace to complete the purchase. That may require opening an account with a particular marketplace if you don't already have one. One thing to note about buying NFTs is that they may not be on sale all the time. In the case of non-fungible tokens for digital artwork, for example, those may only be released at certain times. So before you can purchase a particular type of NFT, you may need to spend some time in the marketplace to get a feel for how it operates. Whether you're buying or selling, it's important to choose a reputable marketplace. And it's also important to consider what you might pay in fees. Some NFT marketplaces may charge a fee for simply using the platform to complete a sale or purchase while others may charge conversion fees for converting your dollars to cryptocurrency.

If you're keen to start your own NFT collection, you'll need to acquire some key items:

First, you'll need to get a digital wallet that allows you to store NFTs and cryptocurrencies. You'll likely need to purchase some cryptocurrency, like Ether, depending on what currencies your NFT provider accepts. You can buy crypto using a credit card on platforms like Coinbase, Kraken, eToro and even PayPal and Robinhood now. You'll then be able to move it from the exchange to your wallet of choice.

You'll want to keep fees in mind as you research options. Most exchanges charge at least a percentage of your transaction when you buy crypto.

Popular NFT Marketplaces

Once you've got your wallet set up and funded, there's no shortage of NFT sites to shop. Currently, the largest NFT marketplaces are:

OpenSea.io: This peer-to-peer platform bills itself a purveyor of "rare digital items and collectibles." To get started, all you need to do is create an account to browse NFT collections. You can also sort pieces by sales volume to discover new artists.

Rarible: Similar to OpenSea, Rarible is a democratic, open marketplace that allows artists and creators to issue and sell NFTs. RARI tokens issued on the platform enable holders to weigh in on features like fees and community rules.

Foundation: Here, artists must receive "upvotes" or an invitation from fellow creators to post their art. The community's exclusivity and cost of entry artists must also purchase "gas" to mint NFTs means it may boast higher-caliber artwork. For instance, Nyan Cat creator Chris Torres sold the NFT on the Foundation platform. It may also mean higher prices not necessarily a bad thing for artists and collectors seeking to capitalize, assuming the demand for NFTs remains at current levels, or even increases over time.

Although these platforms and others are host to thousands of NFT creators and collectors, be sure you do your research carefully before buying. Some artists have fallen victim to impersonators who have listed and sold their work without their permission.

In addition, the verification processes for creators and NFT listings aren't consistent across platforms some are more stringent than others. OpenSea and Rarible, for example, do not require owner verification for NFT listings. Buyer protections appear to be sparse at best, so when shopping for NFTs, it may be best to keep the old adage "caveat emptor" (let the buyer beware) in mind.

Should You Buy NFTs?

Just because you can buy NFTs, does that mean you should? It depends, Yu says. "NFTs are risky because their future is uncertain, and we don't yet have a lot of history to judge their performance," she notes. "Since NFTs are so new, it may be worth investing small amounts to try it out for now." In other words, investing in NFTs is a largely personal decision. If you have money to spare, it may be worth considering, especially if a piece holds meaning for you. But keep in mind, an NFT's value is based entirely on what someone else is willing to pay for it. Therefore, demand will drive the price rather than fundamental, technical or economic indicators, which typically influence stock prices and at least generally form the basis for investor demand. All this means, an NFT may resale for less than you paid for it. Or you may not be able to resell it at all if no one wants it.

NFTs are also subject to capital gains taxes just like when you sell stocks at a profit. Since they're considered collectibles, however, they may not receive the preferential long-term capital gains rates stocks do and may even be taxed at a higher collectibles tax rate, though the IRS has not yet ruled what NFTs are considered for tax purposes. Bear in mind, the cryptocurrencies used to purchase the NFT may also be taxed if they've increased in value since you bought them, meaning you may want to check in with a tax professional when considering adding NFTs to your portfolio. That said, approach NFTs just like you would any investment: Do your research, understand the risks including that you might lose all of your investing dollars and if you decide to take the plunge, proceed with a healthy dose of caution.

The Opportunities With NFTs

NFTs become a compelling investment opportunity when you consider the art's resale value. It's similar to buying physical pieces of fine art. Having possession over the art itself isn't going to bring you any returns if you are only planning to hold on to it. Of course, staring at that piece of art might give you some sense of satisfaction. But it's selling that piece of art to the highest bidder that brings in the big gains. Put it this way, if you're able to purchase a unique NFT and then potentially sell it for more than what you paid for, you could make a handsome profit. The beauty of blockchain is that no fraud and theft are possible. There will be codes and authentication to prove and verify that piece of art you have. Sure, others can still make copies of an original piece of digital art, but there's still only one original. That person who owns the NFT for that piece of art owns the original.

Are NFT Stocks The Right Investment For You?

If someone asked you what NFT stocks were in January, you would probably look at him or her blankly. Needless to say, the excitement has fueled rallies in countless tech stocks on Wall Street this week. Like I said earlier, some of these have no relation to the NFT niche. But investors presume these companies might gain exposure to NFTs based on speculation. It's really hard to say at this stage whether NFT stocks will take off for good. Look at marijuana stocks and cryptocurrencies at 2017-2019. There's a good chance that the hype over NFT stocks will soon dissipate if history provides good guidance. With all the hype going around, it's easy to dismiss it simply as science fiction that will never materialize. However, if we look closely, you would know that something is brewing behind the scene. And why might I say that? Well, according to data from Nonfungible.com, the total value of NFT transactions jumped to $250 million last year. In the past month alone, NFT transactions exceeded $220 million. It seems like we could be witnessing something growing at an exponential pace.

Advantage of Non-Fungible Tokens

It's only a matter of time before NFTs achieve mainstream status given its massive profit-building potential. It's a wise move to learn how you can use them to fortify your investment portfolio and it's wiser to do that as early as now.

NFTs have the edge over real-world collectables since users can use the blockchain to verify their authenticity or trace it back to the original creator.

NFT marketplaces' presence allows the buying and selling of these assets in a decentralised manner and without a third-party. This essentially lowers the cost of investors.

NFTs are set to solve the inflation problem facing in-game assets, allowing developers to manage these digital economies effectively.

These tokens support real ownership since buyers immutably gain access to the assets. Neither the immutably gain access to the purchased assets. The issuer cannot revoke this ownership for any reason in the future.

Disadvantages

The decentralised networks on which developers build NFTs are not user-friendly. This is a critical barrier to mass adoption since most of the targeted audience for these products know little to nothing about blockchain.

NFTs are not divisible like bitcoins or other currencies. Although this trait is desirable to collectors, it doesn't support inclusion and sometimes inflates assets' price.

The whole future of collecting NFTs hinges on the next generation, placing value on these items and being willing to pay higher amounts for them. Except in cases where the collector has a personal attachment to the article, investing in an NFT could be a speculative and risky investment.

End

NFTs address a new type of digital speculation resource that you may consider as a alternative to claiming tangible assets, such as artwork or collectibles. Before you dive in, it's important to gauge the chances against the rewards to determine if it's right for you. It's a newer phenomenon so it hasn't been tested by time yet. While there's certainly room for growth, it's possible that NFTs could experience the same developing pains as other new investment trends, including rectifications or even a crash. So keep those things in mind as you decide whether to invest. NFTs are turning out to be an energizing offshoot of the crypto and blockchain industry. This article clarified how NFTs work, existing use cases in DeFi, and the advantages and burdens of NFT tokens.

Manufactured by Amazon.ca
Bolton, ON